21 Essential Stories To Take
On Your College Journey

WHAT TO PACK?

21 Essential Stories To Take On Your College Journey

CECIL JOHNSON

Baynton & Banks Publishing

First Printing: 2016

ISBN 978-0-9975353-0-3 (paperback)
ISBN 978-0-9975353-1-0 (Kindle ebook)

Baynton & Banks Publishing

Cover Design by David Kroth | www.kroth.com
Interior Design by Lorie DeWorken | www.mindthemargins.com

DEDICATION

This book is dedicated to those who, at times, wonder:

Am I prepared for this journey?
Am I alone?
Will I be successful?

Yes, you are.
No, you're not.
Yes, you will.

Packing List

INTRODUCTION

Writing this section was tough. How do I write an introduction so compelling that you want to read on? I was told the introduction has to grab the reader, or they won't explore the rest of the book. That's way too much pressure to be perfect, instead I'll be honest.

This book is about honesty, real people, and real experiences for the real world. Some may think college is not the real world, but the decisions and choices you are faced with have very real consequences and those consequences can and will create personal ripples that last way beyond the time in school. This book is meant to help you take control of your ripples.

There is a saying that experience is the best teacher. Some also say someone else's experiences can be an even better one. On the surface, this book simply appears to contain stories, but as you read, you will see they are experiences. Essential ones. Sure, it may seem like I'm just mincing words differentiating "stories" and "experiences," but for the people sharing them, these are very personal episodes that had an irreversible impact on their lives—hence, experiences. So much so that some of the narrators hadn't shared them previously, even with their families, which is why some are signed anonymously or with initials. Yet each person felt his or her particular "critical incident" was important enough to share, and that you were important enough for them to be vulnerable for, bringing their experience to life for you to read. You may ask, why?

While they don't know who you are, at some point, they were you, and they made varied choices, some good, some bad, and wished they had someone who shared an experience to help them. They decided to be that someone for you.

This book is also about getting a head start. I don't presume that it will save you from every challenging situation. But if what you read makes one decision or choice easier or more intentional (and you pause for just a heartbeat more in the midst of that challenge) you will be one step ahead of most people. And if you make a better choice because of that pause, well, you'll find yourself ahead of the game.

I could go on, but by now, you've already decided if you will take the time to read a chapter or two, and I honestly hope you do. There's no need to read in any particular order; just go with what grabs you. I don't think life is all about going "in order"—it's probably more about "going," but hey, I'm still learning.

When I was headed off to college, I was so focused on all the things I wanted to take with me to school that at times

I forgot the important values, principles, and boundaries instilled in me that would be the most important for my journey. My wish is that this book helps you think about what you take with you and carry daily, regardless of where you are in your college career. In essence, it's about answering one critical question: "What to Pack?"

1

A Picture Worth a Thousand Worries

Anonymous

I'd just come out of a relationship that started freshman year and now, as a junior, realized I had been in a type of bubble for two years. I hadn't interacted with many people, meaning girls, because I was so into my relationship. I was a part-time on-air host at the campus TV station and had somewhat of a following and now single, I felt I had plenty of opportunities. It was time to catch-up. Mistake.

I met this girl on social media.

As we "talked" I felt we were making a connection and decided to exchange pictures. When her picture came through, I was like, *Oh, she's going all in. Well, I can definitely play that game…* And I decided to go all in too, actually more like "all out." After a few days, I started to get texts from someone who said they hacked my phone and had the pictures I sent to her. I couldn't breathe, started to shake, my body went cold, and I began to sweat—like the flu. The hacker threatened to mass email all the pictures to everyone on campus and faculty—unless.

He didn't want money; he wanted sexual acts, and he wanted them done on his designees. I was more than scared; I was terrified. A five-second "snap and send" had just blown up my life and now I was in hell. He threatened to expose everything, no pun intended and told me not to talk to the police, not to anyone. He knew my class, work, and social schedule; he told me not to attend an event I was hosting—he had me on a string. My close friends thought it was a scam. Scam or not, he had my phone number, the pictures, and enough information about me that I knew he'd hacked me. I was embarrassed, vulnerable and felt tormented. I walked around in a daze after that; nothing mattered to me except getting out of this emotional prison; I felt trapped and I'd given this digital thug power over me. I was no different than people my age, I knew what cyber-bullying was, but knew it would never happen to me. Now I was living in a *Catfish: The TV Show* episode.

Though it was never an intense thought, I now understood why some people felt the only option was to end their lives. Depending on their emotional state, they may feel isolated, controlled, and hopeless. At different times I felt all those things, but I realized I had options. There are always options.

I decided to talk to the police despite the threats; if I was going down it would be swinging. The police laughed at me at first and thought it was funny! Yes, the police didn't take it seriously and thought it was a joke, but when they scanned my phone, their perspective changed. They uncovered that this hacker was running this scam, game, or whatever you want to call it, on a lot of people—hundreds. The girl I sent the picture to was him! He was also the "designee" he wanted me to do sexual acts with, and had been successful pulling this off with others.

The worst was telling my parents—I was upset and scared that their perception of me would change; no one wants their mom or dad to find out they are in this situation, but I needed their help. I didn't want them to think I was a lost cause and they could no longer trust me. But they supported me, they held me up and let me know they were there for me, would fight with me and that mistakes happen. They assured me that this was something I could and would overcome; it was a lesson that would strengthen me. That conversation, while difficult, connected me back to the person they taught me to be and one that would overcome this horrific episode.

The police were able to track and catch him. He tried to rationalize his behavior as trying to teach people a lesson. Well, he taught me one. I could have required a phone call, then a face-to-face meet up and definitely no body part pics. No matter how well you think you've mastered emojis, it does not replace sitting across from someone.

I learned to raise the standards for who I allow in my life and allow to have a personal and intimate connection with me—analog and digital. Those standards can prevent a villain from turning you into a victim and those standards now separate the person I was before with who I am now.

2

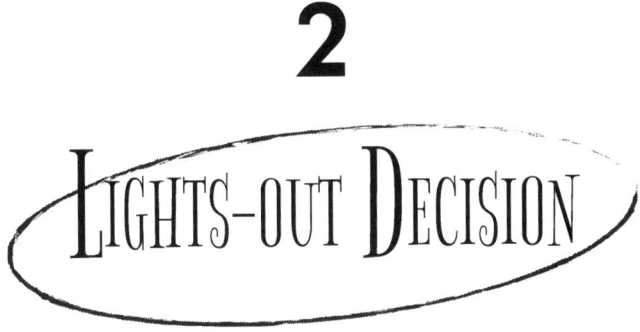

LIGHTS-OUT DECISION

D. Mack

Crazy things can happen during a blackout on a college campus. I'd seen plenty of crazy things before—you can't help not to growing up in West Philly—but I was in my freshman year, down South, and I was supposed to be away from stuff like this...or so I thought. Let me tell you what "this" was.

A hurricane made it's way up the coast and decided to land on campus, taking out all power. After that, the hallways of my dorm started to fill with murmurings about the campus bookstore now being "open" for business. I found myself taking a football-field-long walk toward it with only the moon to light my path—not because I was curious, but because the blackout seemed to answer the question I'd been struggling with: "How am I going to make it through the rest of this school year financially?" The blackout, coupled with the campus bookstore's fallen security system, seemed to be just what I needed. Which, I realized as I approached the store, was not an original idea. Still about thirty yards away, I could see the broken store door and, through it, fellow classmates running wild, dashing in and out like their house was on fire and they had to get that one last sentimental item. But it was not their home, it was not on fire, and nothing was sentimental.

Sure, I tried to rationalize my thoughts—many of us felt the bookstore was walking close to the line of extortion anyway so this was justified. My thoughts were conflicting: "Free books! You can sell them and take care of bills, or at least lower your outlay." Fighting the opposite thought, "This is not you; you know better; you don't need to go in there." The instincts fought each other even as my feet were carrying me toward the bookstore. Then I froze and went into a daydream, one where I saw my mom receiving a call from the dean of students telling her she had to pick her son up, because I had been expelled. I could see the phone pressed against her cheek and then falling to the floor, accompanied by a broken-hearted look on her face. That image told me what I needed to do—leave and go back to my dorm. This wasn't me. This was not what I was taught.

As if on cue, I was awakened by the sound of campus police throwing my fellow, soon-to-be-former classmates to the ground and cuffing them. For some reason, I didn't panic, I didn't run, I just walked slowly back to my dorm. Was it fear that turned me around? Fear of the consequences of what my mom would do to me and the disappointment she would experience? Partly, but it was more that I remembered, in that moment, what she'd taught me before I set foot on campus, and I was reminded who I was, and was not, which was someone bigger than that moment.

3

FIGHTING WITH HONOR

Joan Johnson-Gosier

My parents had me when they were older. By the time I was pre-
paring for college, my mom was retired, and Dad had passed
away years before, which meant she didn't have the means
to help me much. College was tough financially, but I made
it through junior year. Senior year, though, was significantly
more challenging. Still, I was proactive the summer before and
sent almost fifty letters to numerous organizations, including
my sorority, requesting any assistance I could get. I received
one rejection letter after another. Then, to make matters worse,
the school misplaced my financial aid packet, and with the
deadline to reapply passed, I felt I'd run out of options. No,
maybe I still had one. My school had an Honor's College for
top students, of which I was one, with a dean to serve as support and counselor. I was confident she would assist me, a

high-performing student, so you can imagine how surprised I was when her response was anything but helpful.

After I explained my situation and asked for help, she said with the most sincere, counseling tone, "Maybe this is a sign from God that you weren't meant to graduate from here; maybe you should go back to Baltimore and finish at a community college." At that moment, I thought to myself: *Wait, did I hear her right? I'm on the Dean's List, a class officer, an active sorority member, and part of the student leadership-mentorship program on campus. I'm just the type of person this school wants to claim as a future alum, and she's telling me I should just be thankful that I made it this far?* As my face started to tingle with anger and resentment, I told her, "I will graduate from here and get a job making a lot of money, and when the university sends a letter requesting alumni donations, I will remember this conversation!" She then had the nerve to respond by telling me I shouldn't be so petty. Please.

That insulting advice from the Dean caused me to reflect on a conversation I had with my parents when I was twelve. They told me that one day they weren't going to be around, and I would have to learn how to take care of myself. I realized that this was that time, and I had to make a choice: Would I pack up and go home to finish up like the dean suggested, or fight for what was mine, what I deserved, and worked so hard for? I learned that at certain points in your life's journey, you will have to either fight or blame the naysayers. I chose to stay and fight.

I noticed some people in similar circumstances played up their situation and cried the blues to school administrators to get a reprieve to stay in school. I was tempted to follow suit, but instead, I became determined to rely on myself and promptly secured four jobs—yes, four: campus tutor, library work-study aide, administrative intern, and selling World Book Encyclopedias on commission, door-to-door. You heard right, door-to-door. I was a young woman, a college student, selling encyclopedias door-to-door, but I was unashamed and did well enough to be promoted to area sales manager, all as a full-time student. At my peak, still in school and holding down the other three jobs, I made over $1,000 a week in commission. I earned enough to stay in school until other aid came in and still maintained a GPA high enough to graduate with High Honors.

To me, my decision to stay and fight was a defining moment that proved that even if my parents weren't there, I would be able to take care of myself. Had I not been pushed to that limit, I would not have had the experience to prove to myself what I could do at that critical moment.

Have I given back to the school? Yes. Was the Dean just testing me? I doubt it; I bet she actually thought her advice was good. Yet what my parents gave me was more significant than any financial aid, and far greater than the skepticism of one doubting administrator. They gave me a strong sense of self, determination, and an uncompromising will to succeed.

4

COMING INTO FOCUS

Lynn Shareef

My story is not one of focus and hard work in college—at least for the first three years.

I entered with the same attitude and behaviors from high school: Interested in all things outside the classroom, like the next football game, party, and what my friends were planning for the weekend. I was concerned just enough about my grades to have an okay GPA, but certainly not working up to my potential. That hyper-social focus was the only explanation I had for the situation I unknowingly created by my senior year. But it's hard to realize at the time what the consequences of your actions might be, especially when your attention is elsewhere.

In my junior year, I was living off-campus, working at the local Macy's while also attending school full time. In hindsight, this is a combination I do not recommend unless you are highly goal-oriented and focused. I was neither. Both scenarios, working and living off campus, pulled me farther away from my studies. Then, I ran into trouble with a few classes and had the grand idea to drop them (one semester I only carried two courses). Hey, I figured it was better not to fail them, especially since they were in my major, and I had the senior year, right? It didn't occur to me at the time how far behind I was falling, and to demonstrate how I wasn't planning for or thinking about my future, the option of taking summer classes never crossed my mind.

Senior year, I woke up out of my fog and decided to investigate where I stood academically and where I was in fulfilling my requirements for graduation. I realized my investigation should have occurred sooner, a lot sooner. The foolish decision of not taking a full course load junior year meant I was going to come up short in credits if I took a standard one now. Okay, yes, it's simple math, but at the time I was more about being "in" college than being "about" college. While I enjoyed my school, there was no way I could fathom dealing with the embarrassment of staying another year and not graduating with my friends. More importantly not living up to the expectations of my family. I was stressed, a little scared, and angry with myself. Due to my lack of prioritization, I would have to take more than 18 hours of courses, in each semester to finish, which would also cost more money.

So my senior year was suddenly about the business of work I should have done during the previous three years. I learned I could have enjoyed myself just as much and concentrated on the real reason I was there: to grow personally, mature, and graduate. Here's what's interesting: because there was no way

I was going to disappoint my parents or embarrass myself, I focused like never before to ensure I would graduate on time, and because of that earned my way onto the Honor Roll for that year, something I hadn't previously done! What could my four years have been like and resulted in if I'd just had some balance? Would that have been more reflective of what my parents expected of me and my potential? What other opportunities did I not see because I hadn't earned the right to view them? Were there parts of my school experience that I missed exploring because of my behavior?

That experience taught me that our college years only happen once; I should have seen the bigger picture. I did not avail myself of the resources that were right under my nose, like talking to my advisor. I don't even recall her name, but if I'd formed a partnership with her or other advisors, maybe someone with more sense than me could have weighed in on the decisions I was making. I've visited my school countless times since graduation, and I am always blown away by the significance of my time there, the impact on my family, and how the experience became a major building block in my life. Even though I wish I had secured that sooner, I know the process equipped me with the knowledge to create stronger structures in my life moving forward.

5

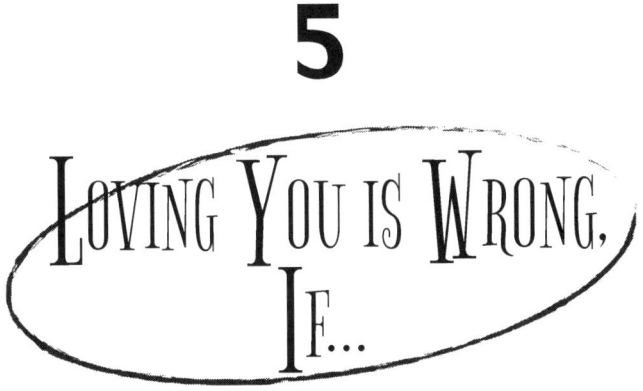

LOVING YOU IS WRONG, IF...

Kevin B.

I was homesick and lovesick.

What should have been a great first year in school became a tough one because of a long-distance relationship and my first time really being away from home.

My girlfriend was not in a good place when I left; she was around negative influences and moved from place to place, living in transitional housing. Imagine dealing with the vision of your girlfriend, whom you love, living in a shelter when you are a couple of hours away. Our relationship was great when I came home, but once I went back to campus, it became rocky. After a few rounds of that, she started to pressure me, letting me know she needed me there, "needed her man with her," and threatened to date other people. She even went on a date with a guy who was always interested in her—but funny how things work out, who did she see while out but my cousin. My girlfriend called me immediately, knowing she was busted and tried to get to me before she thought my cousin could. She didn't.

That put me in an emotional swirl that distracted me and had my stomach in knots. Instead of my head being in my books, it was focused on whether I was a good boyfriend, wondering if she was seeing someone behind my back, and confused as to why I was feeling guilty because I liked the college experience away from home.

I'd determined this girl was "the one," and you know how it is when you think you've found "the one"—everything else is secondary: the world, your world, revolves around the relationship. Yet, I had conflicting thoughts. I wanted to be there for her, but as I said before, I liked school, the classes, my major, and the environment. I'd seen other guys leave school when faced with relationship challenges. They all had good intentions to start school again when at home, few ever did or if they did many flunked out and got jobs. To make matters worse, my relationship issues were hurting the rest of my family.

My mother knew this was a special time in my life, and it hurt her because she could tell I was depressed when we talked. She knew I was torn—moms just know. In the midst of this, my grandmother decided to share some wisdom with me. She said, "There's a lot of fish in the sea. Right now is the fun time in your life, and you're going to school for academics." She told me I needed someone who shared common values with me. Here I was, trying to do the right thing for my future, and my girlfriend couldn't see that or accept it.

My grandmother finally told me, "Tell that hussy you don't want to be bothered with her anymore." Wow! Sometimes you forget that your grandparents have been where you were, and can get real when you need it the most.

At the end of the school year, my girlfriend finished the bit by bit threats and gave me an ultimatum: "I want you to come back home and go to school here, or we can't be together." Funny how that which you think is destiny or love can cause you to make bad choices. Despite my grandmother's advice and my mom's counsel, the pressure from my girlfriend led me to make the decision to transfer to a school back home. Hey, don't judge, I was in love.

As the semester ended, I started packing for the summer, feeling sad and fighting with this sense I was making a mistake. The next day the fight was decided: her ultimatum hit me in a different way. I thought about my parent's hard work and the sacrifices they made for me, my dad's words in his letters telling me to hang in there and persevere when he knew I was going through my emotional ups and downs while trying to excel in school. Then, hearing my mom tell me that regardless of what I do, four years are going to go by, so I should make the most of them, and of course my grandmother's strong words. All of it was like hearing a warning voice in your ear that that tells you, "Don't cross the street right now," and you pause, then a split second later a car zooms past.

When I arrived back home, I told my girlfriend I wasn't transferring. My words didn't end the relationship immediately, but our connection dissolved over time.

I've thought about how different those four years and life would have been had I transferred. That reflection led me to realize that the most important relationship during my time in school was the one between me and my goals and dreams and no one should be allowed to come between them.

6

Anonymous

My dad was an alcoholic; we didn't have much of a relationship, but my high school sweetheart's dad and I had a great
one. He was a good family man, a prominent physician, and
owned properties that I landscaped over the summers for
money. Needless to say, he was one of my role models and
what I wish I had as a father—I cherished my relationship
with him which made the result of a choice of mine so much
more painful.

My girlfriend and I attended colleges in different parts
of the country, and we kept a long-distance relationship
going until her junior year, until she decided to transfer to
my school to be with me, against her family's wishes. It wasn't
that they thought I was bad for her or that we weren't good
together; I believe they felt she shouldn't make that big a

decision over any man she was dating, especially while in college. I loved her, but the long-distance thing was working out just fine for me. Our relationship was rocky at times, but I was compensating for it with my other "friends" at school. For me, this was the best time of my life, and I was acting-a-fool. I had Big Man on Campus status and plenty of women in my life, and even though my girlfriend was now at school with me, my ego stayed just as big, and my extra-relationship episodes did not stop. Until one day, my relationship with her, her dad, and who I thought I was changed.

I found out she'd "hooked up" with another guy at school, and to say I went ballistic is putting it mildly. Sure, it was hypocritical, but as a young ego-driven college student, I couldn't have cared less about the double standard. Even though I was doing my dirt, her dirt, in my opinion, was now reflecting poorly on me (yes, I know it was a ridiculous rationalization). I felt people would think I wasn't in control of the relationship, and I couldn't be Big Man if my girlfriend cheated on me, so I went directly to her apartment to confront her. It was going to be a day of reckoning. What shocked me and made me angrier was her reaction, which I never saw coming.

When I confronted her with what I'd learned, she didn't deny it. Instead, she handled the admission in a matter-of-fact, and in my view, cavalier way. Then, just as calmly and rationally as a lawyer stating the facts of a case, she ran down why she'd done it: 1) my unfaithfulness, 2) how I treated her, and 3) the blatant disrespect. Despite her accuracy, my heartbeat shot up, muscles stiffened, the blood rushed to the top of my head, and I lost it! In a split second, I had her pinned down with a knife in my hand I barely remember getting from her kitchen. I start yelling, "I ought to kill you!" Then, as I looked down at her crying, I felt like I was watching a movie with someone else in it. I was scared to death of the person yelling, pointing the knife at his girlfriend. What was he doing? What was I doing? I just dropped the knife and ran out of the apartment.

The next day I received a call from her dad. He said in a calm, measured tone, "My daughter told me what happened last night; I'm coming down to your school, and we're going to talk." When he arrived, I was scared. Actually, no—I'd been scared from the moment I left her apartment because I knew the call and visit were coming. I was now petrified. Her father came to my apartment and started to talk.

"I'm not sure what happened to trigger this, but I suspect either you messed around, and she caught you, or she messed around, and you caught her. As her father, I have to say you crossed the line, and if it happens again, you'll have to deal with me in a way you haven't experienced, nor want to, but I think it's important I give you some advice.

"You cannot let someone else's actions determine what you do. If in fact, she gave her body to someone else and you let that cause you to do something you couldn't take back, you are at fault because you can't control her, but you can control you. You have to recognize that if you can't manage your emotions and make the right call, someone else or some entity will do it for you and you will not be a success."

His words were so powerful, so wise, and dug so deep that I knew my behavior had sacrificed one of the most important relationships I had, which was with him. I'd let my emotions take control of me as well as not accepting the consequences of immaturely treating someone I said I loved. I paid a high price for that lesson: loss of relationships, knowledge that I could have severely damaged her life and that I would never be able to convince her I was really not that person. I'd committed a terrible act, but I wasn't a terrible person. If I couldn't convince her, I had to prove it to myself—everyday. Every day after that I took advantage of putting distance between who that person was and who I wanted to be. That became the new narrative of my life, and I decided to take control of my emotions so that I could control my choices.

7

VOTE OF CONFIDENCE

P. K. Woodyard

I was in my junior year at Hampton University when I decided I would campaign for the office of Miss Senior. Miss Senior was part of the class leadership council and was required to have sophistication and polish. She wasn't the person you see in a magazine or emerging from a helicopter at homecoming, or being carried by male attendants during a coronation, but she was known and respected by her classmates and was willing to serve. Miss Senior was the position for me!

There is an old saying that weddings and funerals bring the best and worst out in people. I would add political campaigns to that list. For me, my pursuit of Miss Senior was my first major exposure learning who believed in me, who simply backed me, and who would stab me in the back.

I felt I laid the groundwork for my candidacy in the first

three years at school: I was part of the school's student leadership program, a member of the University Choir, and a business finance major with a 3.9 GPA, all which I assumed gave me credibility with my peers. I expected my competitor would receive the majority of her votes from her sorority sisters, but I knew I could draw votes from members of the other sororities and from "independents." Although I had not pledged, I had relationships with classmates across many disciplines and social circles. I studied the campaigns, platforms, and results of our previous class "Miss" officeholders from freshman, sophomore, and junior year. After tossing around ideas with my inner circle, we crafted a straightforward, tightly budgeted campaign. I'd definitely be a tough contender.

We decided to work our plan and didn't consider the possibility that I might lose. Sure enough, on election day, when the polls closed and all the ballots cast, I'd won!

Unfortunately, my happiness was squelched when two things were unexpectedly revealed to me. The first was that one of my competitor's sorority sisters tried to slander me during the campaign. She claimed I was not a team player; that I was unwilling to help others; and that I was selfish and "stuck up" (this last is one of the worst character traits that can be assigned to a young woman in college). Her evidence? I did not help classmates in a well-organized cheating ring. What? What was she thinking? Is teamwork best demonstrated by helping friends do something I know is wrong? Although I thought this person might campaign and vote for her sorority sister, I also considered her a friend—not a close one, but at the very least, a friendly acquaintance who would not purposely sling mud at me.

The second revelation came the night I called to share the

news of my victory with my parents. My mother shocked me when she admitted she didn't think I would win. She thought I surely couldn't have won against a "sorority girl." My mom? My heart sunk and it's tough to describe how disappointed and hurt I was to know that my own mother did not have faith in me, and while she did not discourage me, she wasn't solidly behind me.

Yes, I'd proven my mother wrong and won despite lies and misrepresentation by my opposition, but the victory came at the price of losing some innocence. I experienced a hard fact of life: Some of the people I may count on most will not always be in my corner, and others I least suspect might actively work against me. This experience eroded my somewhat Pollyanna-ish sense of adventure but replaced it with a dose of reality and a strengthened resolve about my dreams and myself. My alma mater's motto is "An Education for Life," and that is definitely what this experience gave me.

8

A LUV NEVER FORGOTTEN

Anna M. Smith

It was my junior year and the Monday after Homecoming weekend. I was on the way to class, walking down the hallway of the business school, wishing there was just one more day to party when I noticed a couple of students to my right talking, with a yearbook open and serious looks on their faces.

As I got closer, being nosy, I slowed down and heard them talk about a student killed in a car accident over the weekend. *How terrible; I wonder who it is?* Then one of them pointed to a picture of Aaron, affectionately know as, "A-Luv." Aaron and I were more than classmates; we were close friends— since high school. *Wait, I just saw him a couple of days ago.* In that instance I had a chilling numbness go from my feet to my head, but still dismissed it, they were wrong.

As I entered class, I started to notice everyone buzzing

about Aaron—dying. Despite that, I continued to reject the thought and left class, though now I felt my heart beating faster and just as I walked out I saw Aaron's roommate walking toward me. *He never comes to the business school; he's a biology major.* I noticed the look of disbelief and shock on his face, which made what I didn't want to believe to be true, true: Aaron had died. I started to feel and hear my heart beating; it became tough to breathe and everything seemed to close in on me.

Aaron and I were close, not in a romantic way, but closer in my opinion. He and I were self-selected brother and sister, and that bond, siblings-by-choice, was very powerful. I was heartbroken in a way that I felt would never heal. The days after became so painful; I cried all the time, which stunned my friends as they always thought of me as the strong one. I was strong, but one of the people who always gave me strength was Aaron and he was gone.

We were a part of a close group of friends that consisted of men and women, and we were all hurting. We learned he was driving at night and hit a patch of fog so thick he thought he was getting off at an exit which ended up being a guard rail. The car went through the guardrail and down an embankment. The impact took his life. If Aaron had his seatbelt on, he might have lived. In college we thought we were invincible, this death did not make sense. Who prepares for such a loss at 19 and 20? You don't know how to deal with it yourself let alone help others. We didn't know what to do, but what did happen was that our definition of friendship changed.

Relationships that were fractured before Aaron's death immediately healed. We learned how fragile life is and the barrier that pettiness can place in front of what is important in relationships. We developed the courage to say, "I love you" to each other as brother and sister. We understood that you never know if it will be the last time you will say it to that person, nor do you know how much it means to that person.

We stood by each other and developed an instinct to detect when one of us was in pain and the uncanny ability to know what they needed. We learned true friendship can stand in the place of grief and at different times we stood in that space for each other. For us, friendship became the ability to minister to someone when they need it and allow someone to minister to you.

When I attended Aaron's funeral, I was in such a fist-clenching, energy-draining sadness that my knees buckled. A woman came over and said something simple, but healing, "It's going to be alright child." I had a choice: to stay trapped in this moment or move through it, paying respect, yet not getting stuck and letting it consume me. No matter how much I did not want to believe his life ended, I needed to keep going.

The loss of Aaron reminded us that at any moment a life could be taken away; yet, interestingly, it also taught us that at any moment life could be given to a friendship. After that, every time we put a seatbelt on it was our way to honor him and our friendships. And every time we told someone to put theirs on, in our way we were saying, "I love you."

9

POP TARTS

Anonymous

We were dressed like we were up to no good—coming from a "gathering" of prospects for our intended fraternity. This particular evening, our not-yet-but-maybe-someday big brothers wanted us to get Pop Tarts. Why? I have no idea. Five of us stuffed into a 1982 two-door dark blue Chevy Camaro Berlinetta and pulled into the parking lot of a Safeway to fulfill the request. We could have scrounged up a few dollars needed to buy them. Maybe even looked on the ground or in the car for spare change, but our collective, collegiate, "genius" minds decided to take a different course: We decided it was smarter to go in the Safeway and take the box of Pop Tarts.

Two went in, one with a big coat for concealment and one for backup. It was late, the parking lot clear and the store almost empty, which seemed like the best time to do the deed, but was actually the worst. Our plan was that "Big Coat" would run in unnoticed, grab and hide the contraband, and run back out with "Backup" close behind. What we didn't bank on was the store manager noticing. Think about it: College kids with roughneck gear on, in a dark car late at night, with two people dressed suspiciously walking in and out of the store, bypassing the checkout line. Who knew? (Yeah, I know). Big Coat came hurrying out and behind him was Backup—and following him was a store employee...one too many people. As they jumped in the car, we still felt the mission was accomplished and were ready to drive off. Well, almost.

Behind us, bright lights seemed to come from out of nowhere and started to heat the back of our necks. A police car! Our college careers flashed before our eyes. Then three other police cars showed up in front of us. *Really? It was just Pop Tarts!* We froze, shut the car off, and as we waited for Officer "Bright Lights" to run the tags, figured we had a couple of minutes to do something. Finally, the getaway driver said, "There's a space underneath the back seat, stick the box in there." (Why he knew that is another story.) As Bright Lights approached our car, we jammed the contraband in the hideaway space; he then asked, well demanded, that all of us to step out of the car. A younger officer then started searching the car while Bright Lights searched us with an audience of officers looking on. Nothing came up in both searches which made Bright Lights visibly and verbally agitated and annoyed. We were now becoming even more palm-sweaty nervous if that was possible. He said, "You took something, where is it?!" We denied it again and again and each time his voice and anger rose as he told us we were lying. Finally, he spoke words in a sinister tone that made us shudder: "It's going to be a long night."

Five smart (before that night) college students, with good grades, from strong moral- and integrity-filled households, simultaneously forgot what their parents taught them. We all knew taking the Pop Tarts was wrong, but not one of us said, "Wait, it's not worth doing this—it's Pop Tarts." No one said, "Suppose we get caught? Let's figure something else out."

As our bodies nervously shook waiting to find out what happens during a "long night," another police car arrived to make the total five. *Great, one for each of us.* Okay, we were wrong, but really—five cop cars? Anyway, this last car contained the sergeant who got out, walked over and looked us up and down, peeked into the car with his flashlight, and asked Bright Lights and the young one, "Did you find anything?" Reluctantly, they said "no", and before they could get out a "but" he turned to us and said, "You can go."

Our entire college careers almost gone, or at least arrested (pun intended), because we forgot to bring with us the good judgment we'd displayed so many times before. Our parents didn't ask us to remember to pack judgment; they assumed it was one of the first things we'd brought with us. We were caught up in the moment and that's where decisions really count. I can't say we were perfect after that and didn't make other mistakes, but we did not make that one again. And the incident gave us all one more experience that would serve as a correction point in our lives.

10

MISSING FOR ACTION

C. W.

Vanessa was one of my best friends. She was fun, cool, and spoke her mind—all the time. We were different in some significant ways, but I was raised not to judge, which kept me open to what was good about her; that's how we became so tight my freshman year.

Similar to mine, she had a loving family with successful parents who wanted the best for her emotionally and materially. Yet my thoughts about certain things were different. I knew there were situations I would not put myself in, and some of those seemed to be the very ones she looked for. I wasn't perfect, and I was certainly not a saint, but I knew why I was in school and what my priorities were. My parents raised me to understand my worth and to believe I was able to achieve anything I wanted. In fact, a week after school started,

WHAT To PACK?

I received a letter from my dad reinforcing his expectations of me and sharing his confidence in my ability to be successful. I vividly recall parts of that letter:

"You are starting your adult life now, and you can do or be anything you want. You've got the brains, the charm, and the looks. You've got it all going for you, so set your goals high. Don't settle for being average—be the very BEST. Decide what you want and go get it, girl! Now is the time to start."

That letter reinforced what had been drilled into me during the previous 18 years, and let me know that although I was a few hundred miles away from home, those lessons should still be with me. I came to school understanding my boundaries and that they would be tested, but I was ready; I just happened to now have a friend who didn't have as many boundaries, and some were different. So despite all the things that I liked about her, the things that made us tight, it was those differences that made being her friend a challenge at times.

Vanessa was always in party mode. She loved to indulge. Okay, I'm just being nice: she loved sex and drugs. She loved men, and she'd let men— lots of men—love her. She would smoke weed, drink whatever, meet a stranger or two and sleep with them—one-night stands and weekend flings were a standard for her. I guess you'd stay she was reckless. I was far from that. She preferred to party instead of going to class and would want me to hang with her, but I made my priorities clear. I had fun and was fun, but I also knew what my goals were. Everything else was secondary. She would test me at times, saying, "I met these two guys, let's…" But though she asked, she knew that wasn't me. More importantly, I knew that wasn't me; I knew what situations I would not be put in.

To cap it all off, Vanessa had a ferocious tongue. I watched her cut people down to the core and think nothing of it. If something or someone set her off, it was tough to get her to back down; she would go from zero to sixty in a verbally piercing second. I tried my best to influence her in the right direction—this was my girl after all—at times I was able and at times I wasn't. So, I'd wonder, "What if I'm not there to save her from herself?" Then Vanessa went missing, and I had a horrible feeling that this was different than previous times.

She'd met two guys on campus, who didn't attend our school, but still decided to hang with them—this was a Wednesday, not her usual weekend excursion. By Friday, we hadn't heard from her, didn't know the guys she was with and had no trail to her. Our dorm and campus were on high alert, and Vanessa's parents had been contacted and were on their way. My imagination went wild because I knew she liked to party, but I also knew that if something didn't go the way she wanted, her fierce mouth might take over, and who knows how those guys would react. This time, her actions were impacting others; we were all worried sick.

Those of us in her dorm decided to hold a prayer vigil, hoping to do something that would bring her back safely. I kept thinking the worst and, knowing her recklessness, felt sure she would be found somewhere instead of walking back into our lives. Day four arrived, and we were consumed with Vanessa's crisis, waiting for some resolution to this drama, which finally came.

I guess Vanessa decided it was time to return, so she did. Just like that, with no regard for the people who'd worried, prayed, and cried over her. Was she regretful? Not at all. In fact, she appeared to be oblivious to and unfazed by the level of distress she caused and wondered what the big deal was. Well, her parents let her know just how big a deal it was: they unceremoniously took her out of school and took her back home to stay.

Through all of her irresponsibility, Vanessa taught me something or reinforced something I knew about myself: The boundaries I set were not to exclude fun from my experiences, but to ensure success from them. I was a responsible, purpose-driven, strong woman who could have fun and excel, and I owed excellence to my family and especially to myself.

11

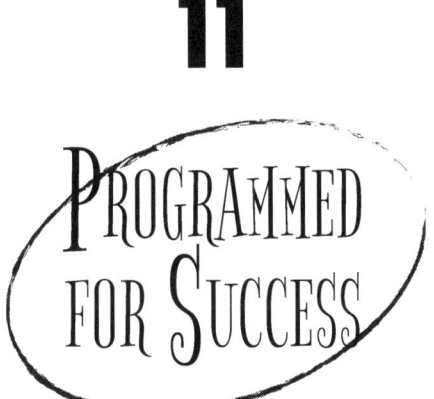

SLJ, CPA

Potential business and accounting majors were a dime a dozen at my school because so many students wanted to be admitted into the prestigious School of Commerce (Comm School). Those majors resided in the Comm School; acceptance occurred in the junior year and before that you had to take and pass courses designed to weed out the weak students. If you didn't pass these classes, the school assumed you couldn't cut it in the Comm School, so there was no need to apply.

In my freshman year, I was full of hope and focused on my goal of majoring in accounting, entering the Comm School, and later becoming a Certified Public Accountant (CPA). Then came a challenge in a computer science class that could have changed the course of my studies.

Computer science technically wasn't a business course, but it was an integral part of the curriculum and a definite weed-out course. It was one of the doors I'd have to go through to get into the Comm School. If I didn't pass, I would have a slim chance at admission, and my purpose at school would all but disappear.

In class, we were given a particularly challenging program to write as an important assignment. I was doing well in the class and usually didn't need help, but for this assignment, I decided to put in extra time in the computer lab and the assignment was now due. When I walked into the building, there was a long line snaking down the hallway and around the corner of the lab leading to the tutor's office. Tutors were there during designated office hours to provide help to students, and the general rule was, the tougher the problem, the longer the line. I was a little stuck on this problem and decided I would subject myself to the wait. I knew I was close to a solution, but wanted confirmation I was on the right track and hung tough in line for forty-five minutes. Now it was my turn.

I don't know if the thirty people before me wore him down, or I was so close he couldn't flex his Comp Sci muscles, but the tutor's reaction totally caught me off guard. He looked down at my work, then up at me, and arrogantly said, "Oh, you're just, like, way off!" I thought, *Excuse me? Maybe I heard him wrong. Why would he say something like that to me? Did he talk to everyone else like this?* As my eyes started to well up, he tried to soften his words, saying, "Well, maybe you're not that far off. It's not that bad." Even though his comments upset me, I rejected them. I knew his assessment was off, and I decided to pack up my things and go back to the computer lab to figure the problem out myself. Committed to staying as long as I needed to get it right, I told my friends with me if they were hungry, we'd need to order a pizza and have it delivered here because I was solving this problem, tonight.

I was close; I knew it, and there was something, just one little thing, I needed to figure out. The tutor was wrong, and I was going to prove it. I moved from being upset to determined. *I waited in line all that time for this stupid guy and he couldn't help? I'll show him.* I went through the assignment line by line, made little tweaks, then decided to press "enter" and run the program to see if it worked. Solved... in five minutes! We were will still figuring out what toppings we wanted on the pizza.

The next year I was accepted into the Comm School, later graduated, and became a Certified Public Accountant, making my dreams come true. My inner voice told me I was close, told me I knew what I was doing, and just as important, helped me discern who was there to help me and who wasn't. This same voice led me to encourage myself, have confidence in my abilities, and tune out "noise" that would try and tell me different.

12

A. W.

College was a given, or at least I thought it was, so I prepared diligently in high school, excelling academically. More importantly, my mother said I was going, which signaled to me that it was a done deal. Unfortunately, I soon learned that paying for college wasn't and when that reality hit me, I had to look for a different way to get what I wanted.

The thought of going to college disappearing due to a lack of money wasn't something I was ready to accept, but I realized I needed to rethink my plan. I wanted to go south for school but didn't want to go so far away only to get stuck in between semesters, without money to get back and forth. Being a first-generation college student, I felt no one in my family could help or understand me. None of my advisors or counselors at school looked like me, so I didn't sense they had my best interests at heart.

Finally, I decided the new plan would be to go the civil service route and take the FBI exam. I still had the dream of going to college and felt the FBI job would help fund it, and I passed and was offered a position in Washington, DC.

One morning as I was about to leave the house, my mother was sitting at the dining room table drinking her first cup of coffee and smoking her breakfast cigarette, looking pensive. She asked what I had decided about college. I told her I'd changed my mind: "I don't want to go." I told her that without money or a support system, I didn't want to be dependent on other people for my basic needs. I shared my alternate plan, thinking my logic was sound.

My mom and I had talked about important things before and she was the straightforward type, but what she said next and the finality of her tone surprised me. She said, definitively, "Sit down. You are going to college! Pick a school; I don't care which one it is, but you will pick it. Pack your little bags (I knew when she said certain things of mine were "little" she was serious) and go. I know you're graduating this year, but you're not 18 yet, so I am still in charge, and you are going to college! If you start working, you'll never go to school. You'll start making money, buying things, getting bills, and having babies" (I'm not sure how she jumped from bills to babies, but I got the point). She went on, "The financial aid papers are filled out, and you should be eligible for some grants and maybe scholarships. We may have to take out a loan, but you will have the money, no excuses."

Okay then, I guess I'm going. In so many words, that was her last, "'cause I said so" moment with me. I was upset, not because of her tone, but because even though I'd be going to college the question still out there was "where." I was also bothered because I had to accept also that it was not going to be down south where *my* school was and it was now April.

I decided to attend a local college and had a funky attitude about it. But after a while, I warmed up to the local school, started to make friends, and loved my classes. It was the best decision I—I mean my mom and I—made in my life. But this decision had other implications, too.

When I told my family and friends I was going to work for the FBI, it was ok—they really seemed to accept it—but when I said I was going to college they changed their acceptance. Some said I became "stuck up" and accused me of thinking I was too good for them. That let me know I may not have the right people weighing in on the path I'd chosen for my life.

Although I was only a few miles from home and lived on campus, I decided I was not going to deal with being teased and listen to how others thought I'd changed, how I talked "white" and acted differently now. I did not go home for months at a time, and when I did, I started to feel like an alien having trouble relating to some of my friends and family. Once I realized that my standards, values, and morals were different from those of many whom I loved, I had a hard choice to make. I still loved them but learned that sometimes you have to cut people from your life in certain ways if you're going to be true to yourself.

I successfully finished undergraduate cum laude and later went on to earn a Master of Science degree. Education opened a new world of possibilities for me, and I now knew who I was and who would have a voice and a vote in my life. If their values were different than mine, they received neither.

13

Dispensing with Doubt

Cecil W. Johnson, Jr.

I was in my second year of pharmacy school at a prestigious, tough institution and felt I was struggling academically while knowing my wife and I were in trouble financially. I usually got better grades and I felt I wasn't cutting it. Things were not going as I planned, sub-par grades and not enough money for school. *Maybe I wasn't meant for this?* Growing up, I was held to a high standard of excellence. When I was in high school, the local paper published each week the names of students who made the honor roll, and every week my mother expected to see my name. I never let her down, and it was the foundation for the high standards I held myself to; now, I was disgusted with my results and felt I might need to withdraw.

I decided to confide in my boss at my part-time job; he was someone who I respected and who always looked out for me. I shared with him the trouble I was having and that I was considering withdrawing and working more hours. My boss asked me if I was passing everything, which I was, but passing wasn't good enough for me. He said, "You're passing everything? Look, you will always have a place here, but as good as that school is, you couldn't drag me out of there." Still, I felt that only passing everything wasn't good enough and that the school would question my abilities. It may not have helped that my journey to college was different from most.

I'd been in the military and was an older student. I entered the school in my first year as a microbiology major and planned to become a medical technician. Two of the people I worked with in the lab during my first year, Morey and Marty, were graduate students, and when I told them of my plans, they said I shouldn't go to school just to be a technician—I could always do that. They shared with me that, "with your brains, you need this," and each pulled out his pharmacy license. After that, feeling I could aim higher, I decided to change my major to pharmacy and requested that the school let me change tracks. The school resisted, stating the competitiveness of the pharmacy major might not be the best option for me. During the first year, everyone takes similar classes, and I was doing pretty well then, so I wrote a "nice" letter asking how my grades compared to those of students currently being admitted to the pharmacy school. Two weeks later a letter came admitting me to the school of pharmacy. Now, in my second year, I wondered if I'd made the right choice and the school had been right.

An example of my school's rigorous academic environment was test time—it was an extraordinary sight to see. During the regular school year, we'd wear white jackets and everyone kept himself or herself in neat and "buttoned up" order—except during examination time. During this time no one cared what he or she wore, if they washed, or how their hair looked. Students looked like death from not sleeping. I knew classmates who would get their last night's sleep on Thursday and stay up until the end of the day Saturday when exams were over, maximizing their study time, often with chemical assistance. For some, it worked out, but others would run out of Ritalin and crash before the exam. It was a fascinating campus phenomenon, to say the least.

Faced with a grueling and competitive environment and ignoring my boss's advice, I decided to make an appointment with the dean of the school to let him know I was planning to drop out. While waiting outside his office, his secretary asked me the nature of my visit. I shared what I planned due to my grades. She said, "You want to withdraw? Are you passing everything (again, with that question)"? I told her, yes, and she replied, "About half of your class is on probation, which means they are flunking two or more classes, and you are passing everything? You don't have any business here today, Mr. Johnson." I guess my appointment was over!

I realized that the standards I'd set for myself were higher than those of the school or of others, and while it is good to have high standards, it is also important to check where those standards are compared to the environment's standards. Doing this sooner would have helped me spend more time achieving with confidence, instead of being filled with anxiety and self-doubt.

Although I now felt better from an academic standpoint, I still had tuition problems looming; my wife and I were still up against it financially. Earlier that semester, I'd written an essay to compete for a scholarship that a pharmacy fraternity gives to students, but that had been weeks ago, and I was not contacted—I needed another solution. During the assembly held to recognize the winners of the scholarship, my mind wandered as I tried to think of a way to pay my tuition. Then I felt what I thought was a tickle, but actually a classmate telling me my name had been called. Yes, my name was called as the recipient of the scholarship! As I walked up to accept the prize in a daze, everything felt somewhat surreal. The scholarship covered almost half of the semester's tuition, which was the exact amount I needed to stay in school. After that, I was able to plan my finances each year to ensure we would not be in that position again. I could have mistakenly withdrawn earlier in the year and not received the godsend of the scholarship. I later went on to graduate in the upper third of my class. I went on to open a successful pharmacy and for years held pharmacy association and society leadership positions.

In school, I was a victim of being so hard on myself that I left little space to feel like I was succeeding or accept that I was; I was manufacturing doubt. There is nothing wrong with high standards, but I put so much pressure on myself I forgot that setting realistic goals still creates the conditions for excelling, which when taken advantage of creates success.

14

MISTAKING IDENTITY

Anonymous

It was my sophomore year, and I was starting to really "get" school. I had a flow that allowed my studies and social life to work well together. I, a biracial Jamaican, the product of a black Jamaican mother and white British father, always found solace in a student group from all over the Caribbean, simply named, the Caribbean Club. The group was responsible for exposing folks to Caribbean culture, promoting diversity and inclusion on campus, influencing the university on student matters, and of course, we knew how to party. My weekly social connection with other students of Caribbean heritage was my recess – playing dominoes, finding the local 'patty' shops in Boston, and going to the local college 'Soca' (Soul and Calypso) parties. All of that gave me a sense of security and taste of my home sweet home Jamaica.

WHAT To PACK?

Coming into the year the club had an opening for the position of president, and I was excited to put my hand up as a candidate. I was even prouder to see my name written on the slate—until that day during a club meeting when Tracey Fuller, a woman I always got along with, decided she needed to tell me something she'd been holding back. She said, "You can't be the president of the Caribbean Club; you're not black enough. In fact, you're a watered-down-white-girl-from-Jamaica who is confused about which club she should be in—period."

"What you say?!" I thought. The hurt that went through me in that instant started with my heart feeling like it was pounding through my chest, then my stomach dropping like I was on a rollercoaster ride. I was gut punched. Then, my adrenaline kicked in, and the blood rushed to my face, and the yelling started. Back and forth with Tracey, then sides were taken between club members. What played out was something that had been lurking beneath the veneer of this club I'd come to love. In that instant, a part of my innocence was taken away.

Tracey didn't want to lead; she just rejected the notion of me doing it. Tracey grew up in New York; her father was African-American, and mom was from Haiti. Tracey had beautiful dark skin, wore her hair short and spoke with a strong New York accent. I looked almost the opposite with my fair skin, straight hair and strong Jamaican accent, but in my opinion, no less Caribbean, but to her, because of my mixed "race", I was unworthy to hold this position. This ignorance was now visible and began dividing the club. I never thought I'd have to deal with something like this, here.

After that I started to question myself, "Am I Jamaican enough? Am I black enough? Why would she pick on me? Was

I sending a negative signal I didn't know? Maybe I shouldn't be leading this group. Is Tracey right?" While I presented myself as strong at that moment, I was intimidated, and self-doubt crept in. I decided not to run for office, started to distance myself from the club and my school's social scene. I began hanging out at a neighboring university, making friends and only going to class at my school, like a commuting student. I had allowed this narrow-minded person to take away my haven.

I took the rest of my sophomore year to get to know who I was and find out what makes me tick. In that nine-second attack, Tracey made me question myself, but my time away gave me the opportunity to reconnect with who I thought I was when I stepped on campus the first day. I remembered what was instilled in me: that no one can define who or what I am on the inside. I was no less Caribbean than anyone else and deserved to lead. I refused to affirm Tracey's ignorance nor conform to the club's narrow thinking. My confidence, mixed with a hint of rebellion, was back and so was I. I was not going to give in to the destructive force that makes race and identity a dividing factor and I was not going to let anyone back me down. I came back with a fury.

As we say in Jamaica, "Wen coco ripe it muss buss" which translates to "when a cocoa is ripe it will burst," in essence, actions speak louder than words. I was going to take action and it wasn't to be the president of the Caribbean club; that was too small for what I needed to show, do, and become. My sights were set on being elected to the Student Council. This council was the guiding body of all student-led groups. In my pursuit to make a difference not only was I was elected, but also as Student Commissioner. I was now responsible for overseeing all the student groups on campus; any activities campus-wide had to come through me. Then I decided to take the leadership of the Caribbean Club. I turned the club into something better than it was and made the by-laws reflect the spirit of who we truly were.

That year was a growth year for me. The irony was that I joined the club to connect to my identity, and yet I learned that the club or any social circle could not do that for me. I'd allowed someone to give me a label and cause me to question who I was. However, in that questioning, I defined myself, remembered the lessons I'd brought with me to school and took action with them in my heart and mind. I became grounded in who I was, my values and not how I looked, didn't look, or how someone one thinks I should have looked. I was now protected, armed and powerful because I defined me.

15

EVERY REASON TO STAY

Kelci T.

I had every reason to stay.

My best friend had a stroke a few years before and needed a lot of care … my dad. As the youngest, how could I leave him? My mom and sisters were taking care of him, but would it be selfish for me to go? I had every reason to stay—support, love, guilt, and a little fear. My friends were here, most stayed local after high school and my boyfriend, "the one" was here. And to top it all off, my "guidance" counselor told me, "You should probably think about going to trade school." Yet I knew there was something else for me.

In high school, I didn't try too hard academically. I knew I was bright; things came easy to me, and I didn't have to do much to get B's and C's, but I didn't fight for A's. Regardless of my grades, I knew I was going to college; it was a foregone conclusion in my home despite the guidance counselor's idiocy. The question was where.

My dad was everything to me, and when he had a stroke, it changed my life. He was my academic conscience and regulator, vacation-fun partner, and kindred spirit, and he always had the right answers. While I became used to his health being diminished (as much as one can), how could I leave the burden of his care solely on my mother, especially if I had the choice to help? My older sisters were there for support, but they no longer lived with us. It created emotional unrest for me.

I decided to take something of a respite from my decision and enrolled in a community college; I planned to get back to the levels I knew I was academically capable of and then transfer to a four-year institution. Despite taking a slight detour, the question of where I'd go kept returning, and for some reason, it seemed like Atlanta, Georgia, was answering. I didn't have a strong connection there; there was some family, but we weren't very close, and one friend from high school— that's it. However, after a short visit with that friend, I knew Atlanta would be my new home. I came back from that trip feeling different and the love of my life, my boyfriend, knew it. He shared with me that he could feel the change when I returned, and while he loved me, he didn't want to hold me back and knew he couldn't; which later created the space for me to meet the true "one."

I now had to decide which school in Atlanta I'd attend and found one that would provide the greatest opportunity for me to grow. At this school, I would have to make new friends and walk through the doors of a large institution as a stranger (I'd be a sophomore transfer, and the other students would have established bonds from freshman year). But I had bigger dreams that required a tougher personal fight, and though I knew it would be a challenge, it was one I wanted, needed, and was ready to face. When I shared my plans with my friends, too many of them said they couldn't believe I was going by myself. I chalked it up to their naiveté, jealousy, and fear—they didn't have the guts to do it themselves. When I told my parents, they said to go. My mom was always the cheerleader in my life, encouraging me to go after my dreams, and never wanted me to be held back by circumstances at home. It was time to prepare for the next phase of my life.

I knew my decision was the right one, but the night before leaving for Atlanta, I had a major breakdown. I questioned my decision, asking myself, "Why am I doing this? I don't have any friends, support, or a true connection there. I'll be alone. What am I thinking?" My decision was about to become reality, and it was right in my face. I told my mom what I was feeling, and she gave me just what I needed: a hug and the right words. She said, "You're going to be alright, and it's going to work out just fine." After that, I knew it would be—it was my time.

When I arrived in Atlanta, I knew I'd made the right choice, at the right time, for the right reasons. I approached school and life with purpose and different than when in high school. I recognized there were real consequences to the work I did or did not put in and that I'd have to do something meaningful when I finished. I met the right people and surrounded myself with those who were different from me, yet who allowed me to be more than I was—and who are still my friends to this day. I focused on learning the right things, excelled at my studies, and graduated magna cum laude, all while maintaining a sense of adventure and curiosity. I knew this would be a unique time in my life and that I had to give myself permission to go and create a new path. I had every reason to stay; I'll never regret going.

16

RULES OF ACCOUNTING

D. Mack

"Grades will be based 70% on test scores and 30% on participation," declared Dr. Wright, my Intermediate Accounting professor, during the first class of my junior year. Even though he had a reputation for being the toughest and most feared instructor in the Accounting department, I thought there was no way he was serious. Was he implying that I could have a 100% test average and still get only an average grade if I didn't actively participate? Yeah, right, Dr. Wright. Surely he didn't expect me to raise my hand in every class? I learned the hard way that yes, he did.

Little did I know that during each class, he'd put a little "tick" or check mark next to our name every time we participated. He'd add them up and calculate participation scores. No checks, low participation score; lots of checks, high participation score—simple accounting at its best. At the end of the year, the space beside my name was almost empty, and I failed the class. To make matters worse, I lost my Honors designation and, to add insult to injury, Intermediate Accounting was offered once a year, which meant I had to wait until senior year to take it again—and Dr. Wright was the only instructor!

Senior year, I decided my approach should be a little different. For Dr. Wright's class, I arrived 10 minutes early, like a church trustee turning on the lights and unlocking doors; I sat in the front row like a deacon and participated like an evangelist. I'm not saying I'd found religion, but after the "F" Dr. Wright had given me, I was a convert to his rules. In fact, I raised my hand so much and answered so many questions that Dr. Wright finally said, "Young man, that's enough!" I worked so hard that semester and knew the information so well that during the final exam, I found an error in one of the questions, which the professor had to change during the test. My change in attitude and effort earned me an "A" in his class, and that returned me to the Honors designation. Perhaps even more importantly, I learned that even if I do not agree with the rules of play, it doesn't mean I can't excel in them.

17

LIKE A VIRGIN

Anonymous

I came to school a virgin. Well, not exactly; let's say a virgin once removed. Two weeks before leaving for college I experienced my first time, and it was magical—not. It wasn't a beautiful romantic experience like a prom-night memory you'd later brag about on Monday back in school. Far from it.

I was a late bloomer and as a guy, that's tough, real tough. All my friends seemed to get their "manhood" way before me, and I did my best to conceal my "virgin-ness." Yet I was committed to going to college as a man. So I plotted on a young lady and laid the groundwork of teenage seduction to ensure it would happen before I left. Mission accomplished. But I didn't feel any more like a man than before. Now, I did enjoy the feeling, and I knew I'd definitely want to do it again at the next opportunity, but it wasn't special. And it was unprotected. Yeah, I know—dumb, very dumb, and you can imagine the situation I'd now put us both in.

I arrived at school, and it seemed that the primary goal of every male freshman was sex…and, interestingly enough, many female freshmen, too. And as I said, I knew I wanted to do it again, yet my experience left me in a conflicted state of mind, one filled with anxiety, as I was wondering if I'd gotten this girl pregnant. Someone I didn't care about, and it didn't really matter if I ever spoke to again. If I was truthful with myself, I really didn't like her that much. Because of my hormones, pressure I'd put on myself, and peer pressure—which was really fear pressure (fear of being the only one who hadn't done it)—I did not consider that I might be connected to this person forever, which would change the direction of my life.

My entire first semester I thought about that every day. So I came to school not only thinking about the joys of sex but the consequences of it. Meanwhile, all my new friends talked about were the joys of sex it seemed like all the time. So I had to develop a way to be cool, but not weird because I wasn't this sexual hunter like them. My hormones were raging like theirs, but so was my fear. Yes, I knew protection was available, but it was too late for my last encounter and at that moment I needed something to protect my mind.

The entire semester, every time I called home, I'd ask my friends about that girl. To conceal my true concern, I would inquire about a bunch of people and then throw in her name. Each call, my heart would beat faster as I just knew I'd hear, "Oh, her, yeah, did you know she's pregnant?" And before each call, I'd think about how my life would change, the impact on my parents' lives and how disappointed my family would be with me if I heard that answer—every time, all semester long. So much worry and distraction, all due to a few minutes of pleasure and a fake "manly" goal based on what I thought my friends and the world expected of me. At least that worry kept me academically focused because I figured that if this were my last semester, I would prove to myself what I was capable of, so I earned a 3.5 GPA.

When I arrived home for winter break, I rolled through my neighborhood to see my friends and made a concerted effort to casually "bump" into the young lady, who thankfully had no "bump" herself. Thank God! I'd been saved from a situation I could have avoided. I had already succumbed to peer pressure, expectations of masculinity, and I paid for it, but my price could have been higher.

You see, I came to school as the type of person who would not do anything I didn't want to do. Peer pressure was something I had been immune to—and that's what bothered me so much. I'd put myself, and that young lady in a situation I knew wasn't about what I wanted, but what others did. From that point forward I vowed I would do my best never to do anything I didn't want to do, regardless of who didn't like me for it, didn't understand me, or teased me about it. I decided I would learn and grow into someone special because my choices, good or bad, would be my own.

18

A.T.

"Unfortunately, the funds have been depleted; there is no longer a scholarship...but we want you to come back." That was the gist of the letter that arrived on my doorstep the summer of my junior year, only a few weeks before the start of school. The letter was courtesy of the University that, up until that moment, I thought had me on a five-year academic scholarship. They were now going back on their word.

I chose the school and program due to the university's commitment and the enticement of the full scholarship. My commitment to the school in return was that I would be an exemplary student. I was delivering on that commitment by ranking number one in the electrical engineering department. I knew there must have been some error; maybe this letter was meant for someone else and I could sort it out with the financial aid department in person.

The financial aid office's wait times were legendary and as I waited for a ridiculous amount of time, I was able to confirm that the legend was true. Finally, I arrived in front of the person who I was sure would fix this obvious error. After explaining the situation, the aid officer looked at me over the top of his horn-rimmed glasses and while shaking his head side-to-side to emphasize his words, he sarcastically said, "Well, look at it this way, at least you got two free years of education. That is more than most kids get." *What?! Was he for real? Is this how you treat your best student, by breaking promises?* Unfortunately, he was serious, and I left the office feeling the way someone does when they've been scammed or let down. I didn't have many financial options. My parents did not have any money to pay for school and while I had a solid summer job and saved, it was nowhere near what I would need to get through this semester. I knew I could apply for financial aid, but it would not come in time for me to start the term, so I planned to leave school, work to make the money I needed to return, and evaluate if this was the right place for me.

I lived in an apartment off campus that I usually kept all year round, but now I had to pack my bags and head home. While talking to my mom, she encouraged me to stay positive, pray for solutions and something would happen. That encouragement led to a spark and I declared, "I'm not leaving here! I am destined to do more than this, and I won't lose this semester. I've got things to accomplish that I'm not willing to sacrifice." I immediately started working out my options.

My summer job was a great internship at a major company, where I performed so well they committed to me for the next summer. I decided to call my internship supervisor, explained my situation and asked if they had any scholarships. What did I have to lose? When we talked, he said, "Let me see what I can do." In just a few days, I received a call from the dean of the engineering department telling me they had a full scholarship waiting for me—for the remaining three years of my five-year program.

I often wondered why things happened that way. The school I trusted, which never told me funds could run out, was willing to leave me hanging. Though I was very angry, disappointed and hurt, I packed faith. I wasn't sure where I was going to land and how I would get through, but I believed there was an anointing on my life and success was imminent. I believe everything happened exactly the way it was supposed to, and the experience taught me that everyone you touch could play a vital role in your success.

19

GROWING CONFLICT

Elaine L.

I was so excited to be accepted to my mother, uncle and cousins' alma mater—I was following in their footsteps! I was even more excited to have one of my best friends as my roommate. That summer, we talked about everything we'd do when we got to school. We even went shopping together with our mothers so the things in our room would look cute matching. This college experience together was going to be great!

By October, the second month of school, we were at each other's throats. My friend has always been a very neat person. Me, on the other hand—not so much. That difference wasn't an issue back home, but now we were living together, and I tried to keep my things in order, but I just couldn't do it. We started spending less time hanging out with each other and began hanging out with our new friends more often. We started to fight with each other all the time and talk about each other to our hallmates. I think I became jealous of her because she was making new friends, and she was jealous of mine, too. I mean, this was my best friend! Her friends had to be my friends and mine, hers; as far as I was concerned.

It became more and more difficult to live together, with one argument after another, until one day, we had a big public blow-up because she wore a pair of my shoes without asking. We had worn each other's clothes before, but she didn't ask this time, and the fact that our relationship was already on the edge, this "violation" took things to another level. Our solution during our heated attempt to resolve the situation was to put a tape line down the middle of our dorm room floor: her side, my side. The tension in our relationship put my stomach in knots every time I walked in the room. Many nights, I stayed with other friends just to avoid the conflict, and we both began to realize that we could not live together any longer.

Everything finally came to a head in March when our hallmates had to step in and mediate our feud, can you believe it, an intervention in college! We gathered in another friend's room and talked—well, argued—about what the other person was doing that made each of us angry. I realized that I thought I should be her only friend, but I could have as many friends as I wanted. Even then, I had to admit that was ridiculous. I also felt left out from what was happening in her life; we didn't talk the way we used to and I had a tough time accepting that I was not her only confidant and that someone else was taking my place. I found out that she'd already planned on rooming with another one of our friends the next year, which was a shock to me and that friend's roommate, too (who happened to be her best friend from home also). At the time, I was devastated.

Being an only child, I'd never had to share my space before. I didn't know how difficult it could be, not only to share physical space but relationship space and watch someone I was close to create a life without me. This situation, painful as it was, helped me realize I needed to learn how to live with other people and share the same space, both literally and figuratively, in their lives.

So much happened in that conversation. I came to the realization that I was growing up and growing away from my friend and she was doing the same. I don't think either of us thought that we would stop depending on each other, but we knew we couldn't live together and stay good friends.

My roommate and I decided to work on our issues and compromise so we could finish the school year without killing each other. Interestingly, I became good friends with the current roommate of the girl who would later room with my friend, and we decided to become roommates the next year.

As difficult as my "roommate breakup" with my friend was, it taught me some critical lessons. Notably, I need to talk through issues with the people involved, not outsiders, no matter how hard or uncomfortable that may be. That experience and the process of maturing left me with two best friends to this day, along with a lesson in personal change and growth.

20

REWRITING HIT-STORY

Anonymous

You know that old saying, "There were two hits during the fight...me hitting him and him hitting the ground"? Well, there were three in this one, but the first two hits weren't nearly as hard as the third.

It was my last year as an electrical engineering student in a five-year program, and my second full year as a member of a Greek letter organization. That year, a former classmate of mine was starting my fraternity initiation process through the local graduate chapter. I was a little bothered, as it seemed he went out of his way not to speak to me. Why, I don't know, mainly because I felt he should have gone out of his way to be friendly, as he was aspiring to enter *my* fraternity. So in my arrogance, I told him, "After you complete the initiation process, you best not wear any paraphernalia on my yard."

Calling it my yard seems a little presumptuous now, but at the time, I felt justified.

Time went by and he was initiated. One day, when I was visiting a mutual friend, he knocked on the door wearing a shirt that had the largest Greek fraternity letters I'd ever seen—my Greek fraternity letters—and it was like he was throwing it all in my face. So I asked him if we could "talk" outside about his apparent misunderstanding of my earlier direction. Perhaps he'd forgotten; I wanted to give him a chance to display some level of contrition. I asked him to remove the shirt he was wearing; he said he couldn't and wouldn't do that. Okay, then. I told him to take off his glasses. He said he was not going to fight me, and this went back and forth until I ended the conversation with a punch to his face. Hit one.

Did I feel good about protecting "my yard?" I guess I did, as I acted as the defender of all that is pure and just in my organization. Were the founders of my fraternity humming our hymn as they watched my gladiator-esque prowess from on high? Would my fellow brothers respond with, "Man, that's just what I would've done!" or "You did what?" As I reflect, the latter seems to echo in my memory.

He was right: he didn't fight me, physically, but he did fight back when he told the school administration of my actions. Hit two.

As powerful as my right cross felt against his jaw, the left hook of the school's administration was much more devastating against my academic chin and that blow knocked me out of school—I was expelled. Hit three. Now I was tasked with explaining the expulsion to my parents.

My mom was an educator, and my dad, a career diplomat (who never needed to raise his voice because his presence was so strong and intense, the walls shook); both had high standards of achievement and behavior for me. I called them and decided not to sugarcoat the situation. Instead, I shared the entire story, admitting I was wrong. They condemned my behavior, and the disappointment in my mother's voice was worse than the pain of getting kicked out of school.

Then, they inspired me. Together, they told me that telling them the truth and taking responsibility for my behavior was the right thing to do. They proceeded to share with me stories about their younger days, explaining the events that had created defining moments for them and assured me that we were going to get through this together. My mom told me I was an adult now and that the consequences of my actions would be much different than when I was a kid. My dad said, "We're going to get through this one way or another, and you've got to look at this as only a chink in your armor; you're still going to do great things."

I'd exercised bad judgment, which was inexcusable, and was expelled with a 2.75 GPA, bruised ego, and unfulfilled potential. But I was determined to create a different ending to the story I'd written. I transferred to another school, one with a more established and highly regarded engineering program, and my new story began. I took my studies extremely seriously, graduated with an undergraduate GPA of 3.7, and went on to complete my graduate work with a 3.8. I allowed my emotions, ego, and immaturity write my first story, but let maturity, humility, and focus write the second.

21

Rhonda B.

I knew I'd go to college; my parents talked to me a lot about it—a lot. Despite that, I didn't see much reason to rush it, nor did I appreciate how special the opportunity was. I wanted to discover a little bit of life and figure things out for myself. So I decided I'd delay going, work, and make money first—hey, if things worked out, maybe I wouldn't have to go for at least a year or two. I didn't understand at the time how that decision would affect the rest of my life.

It was October, a rainy Halloween night; I was not in school and was just enjoying what I thought life was meant to be when a friend and I decided to go to a party. While driving there, my car got a flat. Luckily, we were near a gas station and convenience store, and I was able to call my dad for help. He said to wait—he was on his way. While getting soaked and increasingly impatient, we were greeted by a gentleman who said he would change the tire for us, a good Samaritan who worked for the highway's emergency crew. I called my dad to tell him; he said to be careful and do not get in the car with the man, then repeated that he was on his way. Meanwhile, the good Samaritan was having a tough time taking the tire off, and decided to give up. He said he could take us to another gas station up the road to get help and before I could respond, my friend jumped into the back seat of his car. I know my dad warned me not to, but I couldn't leave my friend, so I got in the front, but grabbed my umbrella as a weapon, just in case. After all, we'd known this person all of thirty minutes.

As my dad was on his way to the original gas station, he drove past a pretty bad accident surrounded by ambulances and police cars, but kept driving because he didn't see my car in the wreck and was relieved to know we'd be at the station where he'd said to stay. When he arrived and saw my car there without us, he raced back to the accident. There, he saw his worst fears come true.

After my friend and I had jumped in the car, the rain started to pour, and the good Samaritan started driving faster. As we attempted to cross a bridge, the car hydroplaned and at that moment, I knew we were going over the side. Somehow, miraculously, we didn't—another car stopped us from going over by hitting us head on. After the collision, all I remembered was a turquoise ring on the hand of the man who reached in to cut me out of the car. As I felt the rain striking my face, I heard him say, "Hold on, hold on, you're going to make it; it's going to be all right." I was put in an ambulance with a broken pelvis and severe head and neck injuries. My friend broke her back and legs, when my seat dislodged due to the impact and landed on top of her.

When I reflect on that night, when my dad said don't get in the car and my friend did, I had three choices: 1) get in; 2) get in with a weapon, or 3) tell my friend to get out and just wait. No matter how I look at the first two choices, they still go against my dad's warning. That one decision changed my life. I lived with extreme pain from a broken pelvis, and I could have lost my life. My head injuries were such that I had to learn history all over again; I couldn't remember what I learned in my high school or the names of my teachers. I was in horrible pain for almost seven months, but the experience taught me that life was precious and that going to college was an honor and privilege. Not being able to go made me want it more and at the same time I developed gratitude for life, even through the daily pain, months stuck in bed and more months of physical therapy.

Through a long and painful journey, my friend and I healed. We both went on to college, graduated, and have very successful careers. Despite the challenges, I still feel thankful for learning and for the opportunity to expand my God-given abilities. Though I did not remember some of my past after the head trauma, I knew that waiting for me was the chance to begin a future with the blessing of being able to walk and use my brain.

Today, I have daily reminders of that blessing, some in the form of pain, but also in being able to take a breath. Both remind me of the choice I made back then and how lucky I am to be alive to take full advantage of what life has to offer. Gratitude is what I packed for school and now carry with me every day.

WHAT WILL YOU PACK?

WHAT WILL YOU PACK?

❑

❑

❑

❑

❑

❑

❑

❑

NOTES

NOTES

NOTES

ACKNOWLEDGEMENTS

There are many people who have knowingly and unknowingly been a part of my journey in completing this book. However, I'd like to take time to especially thank the people below:

- All of the storytellers for their courage, insight, strength and trust in me with their experiences.

- My wife Shawna, who allows me to be imperfect everyday.

- My children, who make me want to be a better person and challenge me to think differently.

- My parents, who created the space for my curiosity to grow and flourish.

- My brother, who has always been an active supporter of my creative pursuits.

- My grandmother Nannie, who lived her life as a model of *What to Pack*.

- To God, who instilled in me an insatiable creative curiosity that challenges me to change personally and to change the world.

About the Author

Cecil Johnson is a connector. A connector of concepts, ideas, and most importantly people. He is known for his creative approach to storytelling that inspires self-reflection and allows for personal discovery. He has taken this same approach in *What to Pack? 21 Essential Stories to Take on Your College Journey.*

Passionate about removing obstacles and boundaries, Cecil is committed to paying forward the support he has received in his life to help others achieve their goals. He and his wife run a 501 (c)(3) organization, the Athena Educational Foundation, that provides scholarships to college-bound students. A percentage of the profit from *What to Pack?* will go toward those scholarships.

Cecil has a BS in Business Management from Hampton University, and an MS in Organizational Dynamics from the University of Pennsylvania. He resides in Pennsylvania with his wife Shawna and their two children.

Connect with Cecil to share your story for the next installment in the *What To Pack?* franchise, give feedback or become a part of the *What To Pack?* community.

cecil@whattopackforlife.com

43895862R00063

Made in the USA
Middletown, DE
22 May 2017